14. "The Vegetable Garden"   61

15. "The Magic Paintbrush"   65

16. "The Little Baker"   69

17. "The Neighborhood Cleanup"   73

18. The Unexpected Guest   77

19. The Best Christmas Ever   81

20. The First Snowfall   85

CW01499633

Short stories in English for beginner learners

Boost Your English: Enjoyable Stories for Easier Learning

Language Odyssey

Table of contents

Introduction   9

1. A New Friend in the Park   12

2. The Unexpected Journey   16

3. The Family Picnic   20

4. Learning to Fly   24

5. The Hidden Treasure   28

6. The Lost Puppy   32

7. A Day at the Zoo   36

8. The Magic Recipe   40

9. "The Starry Night"   44

10. "The Surprise Party"   47

11. "The Curious Kitten"   51

12. "The School Talent Show"   54

13. "A Trip to the Beach"   57

Short stories in English for beginner learners

Introduction

Hello, dear reader, and welcome to "English Short Stories for Beginner Learners"! If you're holding this book in your hands or looking at it on a screen, it means you are ready to embark on a fascinating journey to learn and improve your English. You are indeed in the right place!

This book is all about making your journey towards mastering the English language enjoyable and rewarding. But, why is learning a new language, especially English, so important? Well, language is our main tool for communication. It helps us express our thoughts, feelings, ideas and lets us understand others. English is one of the most widely spoken languages around the world. By learning English, you open doors to new friendships, job opportunities, travel experiences, and so much more.

"English Short Stories for Beginner Learners" has been carefully crafted to help you learn English in a fun, exciting, and relaxed way. We believe that learning should never be a chore, and what better way to learn a language than through engaging and delightful stories?

Inside this book, you'll find a collection of short, simple, and captivating stories. These stories cover a wide range of interesting themes and are written with beginners in mind. They are designed to be easy to understand and to help you get used to English grammar, sentence structure, and vocabulary in real-world contexts.

Remember, it's okay to make mistakes, they are stepping stones to learning. Don't rush; take your time and enjoy each story. The most important thing is to have fun while you learn. By the time you reach the end of this book, you'll be surprised by how much your English skills have improved.

Ready to begin this exciting journey? Turn the page and let's dive into the magical world of English stories. Happy reading!

Your opinion counts!

Once you've finished this book, share your review on Amazon.

Your feedback will be useful for future readers.

I look forward to seeing how this book has impacted you.

Thank you in advance for your contribution, and happy reading!

1. A New Friend in the Park

Once upon a time, in a quiet town named Sunville, there was a little girl named Lily. Lily was seven years old, with bright blue eyes and hair as golden as the sun. She loved to play outside and make new friends, but she was often quite **shy**.

One sunny Saturday, Lily's mother took her to the town's beautiful park. The park was filled with green trees, colorful flowers, and chirping birds. There was a playground with a **swing**, a **slide**, and a big **sandpit**.

Lily loved the park. She loved the smell of the fresh grass and the sound of the leaves rustling in the wind. But more than anything else, she loved watching the other children play. However, Lily was too shy to join them.

As Lily sat on a park bench, she noticed a little boy sitting alone on the swing. He looked about her age, with curly brown hair and a big, friendly smile. He was kicking his legs but couldn't get the swing to move very high.

Seeing that he was alone and needed help, Lily decided to overcome her **shyness**. She took a deep breath, walked over to him, and said, "Hi, my name is Lily. Would you like some help with the swing?"

The little boy looked up at her with a big smile and replied, "Yes, please! I'm Timmy. I'm new here, and I don't know how to swing high."

Lily showed Timmy how to swing high by pushing back and forth. She also taught him how to slide without being scared and how to build a big sandcastle in the sandpit. They laughed and played all afternoon. Lily felt happy. She had made a new friend in the park.

At the end of the day, Lily's mother came to pick her up. As she was leaving, Lily turned to Timmy and said, "Would you like to play again tomorrow, Timmy?"

Timmy's face lit up with joy. "Yes, I'd love to, Lily!" he exclaimed. They waved goodbye, promising to meet again the next day.

From that day on, Lily and Timmy became the best of friends. They spent many sunny days playing together in the park. Lily was no longer **shy**, and Timmy was no longer alone. They had found friendship, all thanks to a lovely day in the park.

Highlighted Words:

- Shy: Feeling nervous or timid

- Swing: A seat attached to ropes or chains for someone to sit on and move back and forth

- Slide: A sloping surface for children to slide down

- Sandpit: An area filled with sand for children to play in

2. The Unexpected Journey

One bright, sunny morning, Emily, a young girl of 12 years, decided to go for a bike ride. Emily lived in a small town named Willow Creek, surrounded by beautiful scenery of green hills and a sparkling river. She loved to explore her surroundings.

She put on her blue helmet and jumped on her favorite red bike. "See you later, mom!" Emily shouted, as she began her **journey**.

Emily enjoyed the sound of birds singing and the wind blowing in her hair as she rode.

She cycled along the river, across the bridge, and then through a narrow path that led her to a dense **forest**. The trees were tall, the leaves rustled in the wind, and the forest had a fresh, earthy smell. Emily felt a thrill of **adventure**.

Suddenly, her bike hit a rock and the front tire went **flat**. "Oh no!" Emily sighed, looking around. She was in the middle of the forest, far from home. She started to push her bike, hoping to find someone who could help her.

After a while, Emily noticed a narrow path she hadn't seen before. Out of **curiosity**, she decided to follow it. After some time, she saw something incredible. Her eyes widened with surprise.

In front of her was a new **city** she had never seen before. It was hidden behind the forest, out of sight from her usual paths. It was a beautiful city, with tall buildings made of glass and steel, colorful houses, and green parks.

Emily could hear the sounds of people chatting, cars honking, and children laughing. The city was full of life and activity, unlike her quiet town. She felt a mix of excitement and **nervousness**.

She saw a **bike repair shop** nearby. The friendly shopkeeper, Mr. Lee, quickly fixed her bike and refused to take any money for it. Emily thanked him, promising to return someday with her parents.

Walking around the city, she discovered a charming **ice cream shop**, a massive **library**, and a park filled with children her age. The city was full of new sights, sounds, and smells. Emily felt like she was on an **unexpected journey**.

As the sun began to set, Emily decided to head home. She was glad she had taken the narrow path and discovered the city. As she rode her bike back through the forest, she couldn't wait to tell her family about her **adventure**.

And so, Emily, a young girl from Willow Creek, found a new city all by herself. Her bike ride turned into an **unexpected journey**, a journey that taught her that sometimes, a wrong turn can lead to beautiful places. Emily knew she would visit the city again, and she was eager for more **adventures**.

Highlighted Words:

- Journey: An adventure or trip

- Forest: A large area of trees and plants

- Adventure: Excitement about exploring something new

- Flat: No longer filled with air (for tires)

- Curiosity: A strong desire to know or learn something

- City: A large and important town

- Nervousness: Feeling worried or anxious

3. The Family Picnic

One sunny day, the Johnson family decided to have a **picnic**. There was mom, dad, their son Ben, and their daughter Mia. They lived in a small house with a big backyard in the town of Pleasantville.

They packed **sandwiches**, apple juice, and dad's famous **chocolate chip cookies**. They also packed a big, colorful **blanket**, plates, and cups. The family was excited about their day out.

They chose to have their picnic in Sunshine Park, a large, green park in the center of the town. The park had tall **trees**, beautiful **flowers**, and a big **playground**. Children loved to play there, and adults loved its peaceful atmosphere.

The Johnsons found a perfect spot under a big tree near the pond. They spread their blanket and sat down to eat. The sandwiches were delicious, the juice was refreshing, and dad's cookies were the best.

After eating, Ben and Mia decided to play **catch**. They took their ball and started running around, laughing and shouting. Suddenly, the ball bounced off a tree and landed in the pond.

"Oh no!" said Ben, looking at the ball floating in the pond. It was too far to reach. Just as they were about to give up, they noticed a small, wooden boat tied to a tree nearby.

They looked at each other and then at their parents. Mom and dad smiled and nodded. This was turning into an unexpected **adventure**. With life vests on and oars in hand, Ben and Mia stepped into the boat. They paddled towards the ball.

Meanwhile, mom and dad watched their kids from the shore, proud of their initiative and courage. Ben reached out, picked up the ball from the water, and they both cheered.

After returning the ball and the boat, the kids joined their parents on the blanket. They all laughed and talked about the mini-adventure. The picnic was no longer just a picnic. It had turned into a memorable day for the Johnson family.

As the sun began to set, they packed up their things and headed home. They were tired but happy. The family picnic had turned into a lovely adventure they would always remember.

That night, as mom and dad tucked Ben and Mia into bed, Ben said, "Today was the best day ever!" Mia nodded, smiling sleepily, "Can we have more picnics like this?"

Mom and dad laughed and promised more picnic adventures in the future. The family picnic had indeed turned into a day to remember.

Highlighted Words:

- Picnic: An outdoor meal

- Sandwiches: Food made by putting ingredients between two slices of bread

- Chocolate chip cookies: Sweet treats with small pieces of chocolate

- Blanket: A large piece of fabric to sit on

- Trees: Tall plants with branches and leaves

- Flowers: Colorful plants with petals

- Playground: An area with equipment for children to play on

- Catch: A game where someone throws a ball and someone else tries to catch it

- Adventure: An exciting and unusual experience

4. Learning to Fly

In the small town of Skyville, lived a young girl named Sara. Sara was fascinated by planes. Every time a plane passed overhead, she would rush outside to watch it. However, she had a big fear - the fear of flying.

Sara's uncle Joe was a pilot. He had a small, two-seater plane that he loved to fly. He had often invited Sara to join him, but she was too **scared**.

One day, Uncle Joe decided to help Sara overcome her fear. He said, "Sara, you love planes. Why don't you try flying one? I can teach you."

Sara was **unsure**. She was excited but also scared. After thinking for a while, she decided to give it a try.

The next day, Sara and Uncle Joe went to the local airport. Uncle Joe showed Sara his plane. It was small but looked strong and safe. Uncle Joe explained all the **controls** and safety measures.

Sara felt her fear rising, but she took a deep breath and climbed into the plane. Uncle Joe sat next to her, ready to guide her.

He started the plane, and it began to move. Sara's heart was beating fast. As the plane moved down the runway and picked up speed, she closed her eyes tightly.

"Open your eyes, Sara," Uncle Joe said. "Don't let fear control you. Feel the **excitement**. You're about to fly a plane!"

Sara slowly opened her eyes. The plane was now in the air. She looked around. The town, the houses, the trees - everything looked so small from above. It was a beautiful sight.

"Now, it's your turn," Uncle Joe said, handing her the **controls**. Sara hesitated, but then she took hold of the controls. She was now steering the plane.

She could feel the wind on her face and the freedom of the sky. It was scary but also exciting. She was doing it. She was flying a plane!

After a while, Uncle Joe took back the controls and smoothly landed the plane. Once on the ground, Sara felt a rush of **happiness**. She had faced her fear and learned to fly a plane.

From that day on, Sara was no longer afraid of flying. She often joined Uncle Joe on his flights. She had learned a valuable lesson - to overcome fear, you need to face it.

And so, Sara, the girl who was afraid of flying, became Sara, the girl who could fly a plane.

Highlighted Words:

- Scared: Feeling afraid

- Unsure: Not certain or confident

- Controls: Devices or buttons to operate the plane

- Excitement: Feeling of being thrilled or enthusiastic

- Happiness: Feeling of joy

5. The Hidden Treasure

In a small town named Seaville lived two friends, Jack and Lucy. They were adventurous and loved to explore. They often dreamed about finding a hidden treasure.

One day, while playing in Jack's attic, they found an old, dusty box. Inside the box, there was a faded map. It looked very old, with a path drawn across it leading to an 'X'. The 'X', they knew, marked the spot of a hidden treasure.

Filled with **excitement**, they decided to follow the map and find the treasure. They packed a bag with water, food, a compass, and the map.

The next day, they set off on their **adventure**. The map led them through the town, past the old mill, and towards the beach. They felt like real explorers.

At the beach, they found a large, rocky hill. The map showed that the treasure was hidden somewhere on top. Climbing the hill was hard, but they helped each other and kept going.

Finally, they reached the top. They followed the map and started **digging** at the 'X' spot. After a while, their shovels hit something hard.

They dug around it and pulled out a small, metal box. They couldn't believe it - they had found the treasure! Their hearts were beating fast with **excitement**.

Inside the box, they found old coins, a silver locket, and a small, golden statue. They couldn't believe their luck. Their adventure had led them to a real treasure!

Tired but happy, they packed up their treasure and headed home. When they showed their families what they had found, everyone was amazed. They couldn't believe that an ordinary day had turned into such an **exciting** adventure.

From that day on, Jack and Lucy were known as the 'Treasure Hunters' of Seaville. Their adventure made them realize that sometimes, treasures can be found in the most **unexpected** places.

And so, Jack and Lucy, the young explorers from Seaville, had the adventure of a lifetime. They found a hidden treasure and made a memory they would never forget.

Highlighted Words:

- Excitement: Feeling of being thrilled

- Adventure: Exciting experience or journey

- Digging: Removing dirt or soil

- Exciting: Full of excitement

- Unexpected: Not expected

6. The Lost Puppy

In a quiet neighborhood lived a kind boy named Tommy. He was friendly and loved animals. He always wished to have a pet, especially a puppy.

One sunny afternoon, while walking home from school, Tommy saw a small puppy sitting by the road. It was brown, with a white patch on its face. The puppy looked **scared** and **lost**.

Tommy approached the puppy carefully. "Hello, little one. Are you lost?" he asked. The puppy wagged its tail but didn't move.

Tommy looked around. He didn't see anyone who could be the puppy's owner. He decided to help the puppy. He took off his backpack and found an old sandwich. The puppy quickly ate it.

Feeling better, the puppy started to follow Tommy. Tommy smiled, "Don't worry, we'll find your home."

Tommy thought of a plan. He remembered seeing a poster about a **lost** puppy in the neighborhood park. The description matched the puppy. He decided to go to the park and check the poster.

At the park, he found the poster. It had a picture of the puppy and a phone number. Tommy felt happy. He had found the puppy's home.

He used a nearby public phone to call the number. A woman answered. She sounded worried. Tommy explained that he had found her **lost** puppy. The woman was overjoyed. She thanked Tommy and asked him to wait at the park.

After a short while, a car pulled up. A woman stepped out. She had tears in her eyes as she saw the puppy. The puppy ran to her, wagging its tail.

The woman thanked Tommy. She said, "Thank you so much, Tommy. You're a hero!" She gave Tommy a hug.

Tommy felt happy. He had not only found a **lost** puppy but also returned it to its home. He waved goodbye as the woman and the puppy drove away.

That night, as Tommy went to bed, he felt proud. He had helped someone in need. He realized that you don't need to have a pet to experience the joy of friendship with an animal.

And so, Tommy, the kind boy from the quiet neighborhood, became the **hero** of the day. He found a **lost** puppy and helped it return home.

Highlighted Words:

- Scared: Feeling afraid

- Lost: Unable to find the way

- Lost: Unable to find the way

- Hero: Someone admired for their courage or noble qualities

7. A Day at the Zoo

In the city of Winden, a class of 2nd graders were excited. Today, they were going on a school trip to the city's zoo. Everyone was looking forward to seeing all the different animals.

Their teacher, Miss Rose, was equally excited. She loved animals and couldn't wait to teach her students about them. She told the class, "Remember, we must **respect** all the animals at the zoo. They are all special."

Upon arriving at the zoo, the class was welcomed by a zookeeper named Mr. Green. He gave them a map of the zoo and explained the **rules**.

Their first stop was the monkey enclosure. The monkeys were full of energy, jumping and swinging from tree to tree. The class laughed as one monkey made funny **faces**.

Next, they visited the giraffes. The children were amazed by their long necks and even longer **tongues**. They watched in wonder as the giraffes stretched their necks to eat leaves from tall trees.

Then, it was time to visit the elephant family. The children were in awe of the massive creatures. They watched the elephants playing in the water, **spraying** each other with their trunks.

After lunch, they saw the colourful birds. There were parrots, peacocks, and flamingos. The children were fascinated by their vibrant **feathers** and different songs.

Finally, they visited the lion's den. The **king** of the jungle was lying in the shade, a magnificent sight. The children were quiet, looking at the lion with **respect** and a bit of fear.

Throughout the day, Miss Rose taught them interesting **facts** about each animal. The class was fascinated, learning about the different animals in a fun, **hands-on** way.

As the day ended, the children climbed back onto the bus, tired but happy. They had not only seen many wonderful animals but also learned about their **habits** and **environments**.

On the ride back, the bus was filled with **chatter**. Everyone was sharing their favorite moments of the day. The trip to the zoo was not just a fun day out, but also a day of learning and discovery.

And so, the class of 2nd graders from Winden had an unforgettable day at the zoo. They discovered the wonderful world of animals, and learned to appreciate and **respect** them.

Highlighted Words:

- Respect: Show admiration and care

- Rules: Guidelines to follow

- Faces: Expressions on the front of the head

- Tongues: Muscular organ inside the mouth

- Spraying: Ejecting liquid

- Feathers: Covering of the bird's body

- King: Ruler or leader

- Facts: Pieces of information

- Hands-on: Involving active participation

- Habits: Behavior patterns

- Environments: Surroundings

- Chatter: Friendly conversation

8. The Magic Recipe

Once upon a time, in the small town of Cooksville, there was a young man named Ben. Ben loved to cook. He dreamed of becoming a famous chef.

Ben worked as a cook in a local diner. He made burgers, salads, and soups. He enjoyed his job, but he always wanted to create something **extraordinary**.

One day, while cleaning the kitchen, Ben found an old cookbook hidden behind the shelves. The cookbook was dusty, its pages yellowed with age. It was titled "Magic Recipes."

Curious, Ben opened the book. It was full of recipes he had never seen before. One recipe, in particular, caught his eye. It was a recipe for a dish called "Golden Soup."

Ben decided to make the soup. He followed the recipe exactly. He used fresh vegetables, **exotic** herbs, and a secret ingredient from the recipe – golden honey.

He carefully stirred the soup and tasted it. It was the most delicious soup he had ever had! It was sweet, tangy, and **heartwarming**. He knew he had found something special.

The next day, he decided to serve the Golden Soup at the diner. The customers loved it! They said it was the best soup they had ever tasted. Word spread quickly about Ben's delicious soup.

Soon, people from all over the town started coming to the diner to try Ben's Golden Soup. The diner was busier than ever. Ben was thrilled. His dream was coming true.

News of the magic soup reached a famous food critic. She visited the diner and was impressed by the Golden Soup. She wrote a glowing review about Ben and his **extraordinary** soup.

Ben's Golden Soup became famous. He was invited to cook on a popular cooking show. His dream of becoming a famous chef had come true, thanks to the Magic Recipe.

From that day on, Ben was known as the Magic Chef. He continued to cook with love and passion, always remembering the magic that brought him success.

And so, Ben, the aspiring cook from the small town of Cooksville, discovered a magic recipe that transformed his career. He learned that with passion, hard work, and a little bit of magic, dreams can come true.

Highlighted Words:

- Extraordinary: Amazing or remarkable

- Exotic: Unusual or unique

- Heartwarming: Giving warmth or comfort to the heart

9. "The Starry Night"

In the town of Little Hills, there lived four friends named Anna, Ben, Clara, and David. They were very curious and loved to learn new things. One day, they decided to go **stargazing**.

It was a warm summer night, perfect for their adventure. They packed their bags with blankets, snacks, and a telescope. David, who loved **astronomy**, also brought a book about stars and constellations.

They walked to the top of a hill, away from the town's lights. They spread their blankets on the grass and set up their telescope. As the night fell, the stars began to shine brightly.

David opened his book and started teaching his friends about the stars. He pointed to the Big Dipper and explained how sailors used it for navigation. He showed them Orion, the hunter, and told them the ancient stories connected with the constellation.

They saw many more **constellations** like Cassiopeia, Scorpius, and Taurus. They took turns looking through the telescope, amazed by the beautiful stars and the stories behind them.

During the night, they saw a few shooting stars. They all made a wish, hoping it would come true.

As they lay on their blankets, looking at the twinkling stars, they felt a sense of wonder. They felt small in the vast universe but also felt a part of it.

They talked, laughed, and learned together, under the starry night. They discovered the beauty of the night sky, the mysteries of the universe, and the joy of learning together.

As the night turned into dawn, they packed their things and walked back home. They were tired but happy. They had learned a lot and created beautiful memories.

And so, the group of friends from Little Hills had a magical, starry night. They went **stargazing** and learned about **constellations**. It was a night of discovery, learning, and friendship, under the beautiful, starry sky.

Highlighted Words:

- Stargazing: Observing stars

- Astronomy: The study of stars and planets

- Constellations: Groups of stars that form a pattern

10. "The Surprise Party"

In the small town of Sunville, there was a young girl named Lily. Lily was a kind and loving daughter. Her mother's birthday was coming up, and she wanted to do something special for her.

Lily decided to plan a **surprise** party. She knew it would not be easy, but she was determined. She made a list of things she needed to do.

First, she had to decide on the **date** and **time**. She chose Saturday, as her mother would be home all day. Next, she needed to make **invitations**. She used colorful paper and glitter to make beautiful handmade invitations for her mother's friends.

She also needed to plan the **food**. Lily loved baking, so she decided to bake her mother's favorite chocolate cake. She also planned to make sandwiches, cookies, and lemonade.

The **decorations** were important too. She bought balloons, streamers, and a big 'Happy Birthday' banner. She chose her mother's favorite colors, pink and white.

On the day of the party, Lily woke up early. She quietly decorated the living room while her mother was still asleep. She hung the banner, blew up the balloons, and arranged the streamers.

Next, she baked the cake and prepared the other food. She set up a table with a pretty pink tablecloth and arranged the food neatly.

As the guests started to arrive, Lily asked them to be quiet. She wanted to keep the party a surprise. They all hid in the living room, waiting for her mother to come in.

When her mother finally came into the room, everyone shouted, "Surprise!" She looked shocked and then broke into a big smile. She hugged Lily and thanked her for the wonderful surprise.

The party was a success. Everyone enjoyed the food and the fun games Lily had planned. They all praised Lily for planning such a great party.

And so, Lily, the kind and loving daughter from Sunville, planned a wonderful surprise party for her mother. She showed that with love, hard work, and a bit of secrecy, you can create a beautiful surprise for someone you love.

Highlighted Words:

- Surprise: Something unexpected

- Date: A specific day

- Time: The hour of the day

- Invitations: Cards to invite people

- Food: What we eat

- Decorations: Items used to make a place look festive

11. "The Curious Kitten"

Once upon a time, in a quiet neighborhood, there lived a small, playful kitten named Daisy. Daisy had bright green eyes and a fluffy white coat. She was curious and loved to play around in her house.

One sunny morning, Daisy noticed that the door was slightly open. She saw this as a chance to explore the outside world. She stepped through the door and entered the wide, bright world outside her home for the first time.

As Daisy walked down the path, she saw many different things. She saw a big tree full of birds. She heard them chirping and watched them fly. Daisy thought about climbing the tree, but then she remembered how she once got stuck on the curtain back at home. She decided to stay safe on the ground.

Next, Daisy saw a large, scary dog. It was barking loudly at her from across the street. Daisy was frightened, but she remembered what her mother had told her about being careful around other animals. She decided to stay away from the dog and continue exploring.

Daisy then found a garden full of colorful **flowers**. She sniffed them and chased the butterflies fluttering above them. She was enjoying herself. Suddenly, she saw a **bee**. She was about to chase it when she remembered her mother's words about bees. She knew she should not disturb them.

Daisy's little adventure was full of discoveries. She had seen new sights, met new animals, and learned that exploring can be fun but also requires caution.

As the sun began to set, Daisy made her way back home. Her family was worried but happy to see her return safely. She told them about her adventures, and they were proud of her for being brave yet cautious.

From that day on, Daisy continued to be a curious kitten, exploring and learning. But she always remembered to be careful. After all, curiosity is good, but caution is equally important.

Highlighted Words:

- Flowers: Plants that produce beautiful and fragrant petals

- Bee: A flying insect that makes honey

12. "The School Talent Show"

There was a boy named Ben. Ben was a shy boy who liked to keep to himself. He enjoyed reading books and painting, but what he loved most was singing. He would sing when he was alone, away from the eyes and ears of others.

One day, Ben's school announced a talent show. All the students were excited. Some planned to dance, some to sing, others to perform magic tricks. Ben, however, was unsure. He wanted to participate, to share his love for singing with everyone. But he was also scared. What if people didn't like his singing? What if they laughed at him?

Days passed, and the sign-up sheet for the talent show was filling up quickly. Ben would pass by it every day, his heart filled with a mix of excitement and fear. Then, one day, he took a deep breath, picked up the pen, and signed his name under 'Singing.' He felt his heart race. He had committed to it. There was no turning back now.

The day of the talent show arrived. Ben was nervous. He saw his classmates perform, and they were all so good. He felt a knot in his stomach. But then, he remembered why he signed up - because he loved singing, and he wanted to share that love.

When his name was called, he walked up to the stage. The lights were bright, and the room was full. Ben took a deep breath, closed his eyes, and started to sing. He sang from his heart, forgetting about the crowd. When he finished, he opened his eyes and saw the room full of **applause**. He felt a surge of happiness and relief.

From that day forward, Ben was not just the shy boy who loved to read and paint. He was also the boy with the beautiful voice who loved to sing for others. He learned that stepping out of his comfort zone might be scary, but it can also be very rewarding.

Highlighted Words:

- Applause: The sound of clapping hands

13. "A Trip to the Beach"

It was a bright, sunny day when the Wilson family decided to have a fun day out at the beach. The family of four - Mr. and Mrs. Wilson, and their two kids, Jack and Lily, packed their beach gear and drove to the nearby seaside.

Upon arrival, the children couldn't hide their excitement. Jack and Lily rushed towards the soft, golden sand. Jack started building a large **sandcastle**, carefully shaping towers and walls. Lily helped by collecting **seashells** to decorate it. The sight of the siblings working together on their grand sandcastle was a delightful scene.

Meanwhile, Mr. and Mrs. Wilson laid out the **picnic blanket** and set up the **beach umbrella**. They watched their children play, their laughter echoing along the beach. After some time, the family decided to take a dip in the **sea** (the large body of saltwater). The water was cool and refreshing, perfect for the sunny day. They swam, splashed, and played in the water, having the time of their lives.

After swimming, the family decided to play a game of **beach volleyball**. Even though Jack and Lily were young, they played well and everyone had a great time. The game ended with everyone laughing and cheering, out of breath but filled with joy.

As the day began to end, the family sat down on their blanket, looking at the beautiful **sunset**. The sky was a blend of orange, pink, and purple, casting a beautiful glow on the sea. They watched in silence, the beauty of the moment leaving them in awe.

The day at the beach was filled with fun, laughter, and togetherness. As they drove back home, everyone was tired but happy, the memory of the beautiful sunset still fresh in their minds. It was indeed a perfect day out for the Wilson family.

Highlighted Words:

- Sandcastle: A structure made of sand.

- Seashells: The hard, protective coverings of marine animals.

- Picnic blanket: A large, soft cloth for sitting on the ground.

- Beach umbrella: A large, portable shade structure.

- Sea: A large body of saltwater.

- Beach volleyball: A sport played with a ball over a net on a sandy court.

- Sunset: The time when the sun disappears below the horizon.

14. "The Vegetable Garden"

Once upon a time, there was a young girl named Mia. Mia lived in a small house with a big backyard. One sunny day, Mia had an idea. She decided to turn a part of her backyard into a **vegetable garden**.

Mia started by researching what she needed to do. She learned about different vegetables and the best time to plant them. She found out about **watering**, **sunlight**, and **soil**. With her newfound knowledge, she was ready to start her garden.

Mia's mom helped her buy **seeds** from the local garden store. They bought seeds for **carrots**, **lettuce**, **tomatoes**, and **peas**. Mia was excited. She couldn't wait to start planting.

The next day, Mia got to work. She dug small holes in the ground, dropped the seeds in, and covered them with soil. After planting the seeds, she watered them. It was hard work, but Mia was happy. She was proud of her little garden.

Every day, Mia took care of her garden. She watered the plants and removed any **weeds**. She was patient. She knew that plants take time to grow.

Weeks passed, and Mia started to see tiny green sprouts coming out of the soil. It was a joyous sight. Her hard work was paying off.

Months later, Mia's garden was full of green leaves and bright vegetables. She could see the carrots peeking out of the soil, the red tomatoes hanging from the plants, and the green peas wrapped in their pods. It was a sight to behold.

Mia felt a sense of accomplishment. She had started with simple seeds, and now she had a garden full of vegetables. She realized that just like plants, good things take time to grow and require care and patience.

Mia picked her vegetables and brought them to her mom. They cooked a delicious meal together using the fresh produce from the garden. It was the tastiest meal Mia had ever had, not just because the vegetables were fresh, but also because they were the fruit of her hard work.

Highlighted Words:

- Vegetable garden: A place where vegetables are grown.

- Watering: Giving water to the plants.

- Sunlight: The light and heat from the sun.

- Soil: The dirt in which plants grow.

- Seeds: Small, hard parts from which new plants grow.

- Carrots: Orange vegetables that grow underground.

- Lettuce: Leafy green vegetable used in salads.

- Tomatoes: Red fruits used in cooking and salads.

- Peas: Green vegetables found inside pods.

- Weeds: Unwanted plants that compete with the vegetables for resources.

15. "The Magic Paintbrush"

In a small, quiet town lived a young boy named Jake. Jake loved to draw and paint more than anything in the world. He spent all his free time creating colorful **masterpieces** that made everyone smile.

One day, Jake found an old, dusty paintbrush in the attic. It looked like any ordinary paintbrush, but something about it felt special. With **curiosity** sparkling in his eyes, Jake decided to try it out.

Taking a sheet of paper, he began to paint a bright yellow sun. As he completed the painting, something **magical** happened. The painted sun began to glow and radiate warmth, just like the real sun. Jake was **astonished**.

With a thrill of excitement, Jake quickly painted a small bird. As soon as he finished, the bird fluttered off the page and flew around the room, chirping sweetly. Jake couldn't believe his eyes. The paintbrush was truly **magical**!

Jake thought about what he could do with the magic paintbrush. He decided to use it to spread joy and happiness in his town.

The next day, Jake walked around the town, painting beautiful flowers on the fences, colorful butterflies on the trees, and playful kittens in the park. As each painting came to life, the town turned into a **wonderland** full of vibrant colors and delightful sights.

The people of the town were **amazed**. Children laughed and played with the painted animals, while adults admired the beautiful flowers and butterflies. Joy and laughter filled the air.

Jake felt happy. He had used his gift to create happiness and cheer in his town. He understood the importance of using his talents to help others.

From that day forward, Jake continued to create **magical** scenes that brought joy to everyone. And every time he painted, he reminded himself of the **magic** that lies within each one of us, waiting to be used for good.

Highlighted Words:

- **Masterpieces**: Amazingly beautiful artworks

- **Curiosity**: Being really interested and wanting to know more

- **Magical**: Having special powers or abilities

- **Astonished**: Completely shocked and amazed

- **Wonderland**: A magical and fantastic world

- **Amazed**: Very surprised and impressed

16. "The Little Baker"

Once upon a time, in a sunny town lived a cheerful girl named Lily. Lily loved baking more than anything else. She often helped her mom in the kitchen, **mixing** ingredients, shaping cookies, and **decorating** cupcakes. The sweet smell of fresh baking was her favorite scent in the world.

One day, Lily's school announced a charity **bake sale**. The news filled Lily with excitement. She quickly decided to participate and bake her best cookies for the event.

With her mom's help, Lily started to bake. She carefully **measured** the flour, sugar, and butter. She added a handful of chocolate chips to the dough, her secret ingredient that made her cookies so tasty.

After **mixing** all the ingredients, she formed the dough into small, round balls and placed them on a **baking tray**. With a feeling of satisfaction, Lily put the tray into the **oven** and waited.

Soon, the smell of fresh, warm cookies filled the kitchen. Lily took out the golden-brown cookies from the oven and let them cool. She was happy with her cookies. They looked just perfect.

The next day at school, Lily set up her **cookie stand**. She displayed her cookies on a pretty plate, waiting for people to come. Soon, her classmates, teachers, and even the school principal were buying her delicious cookies. Seeing everyone enjoy her cookies filled Lily with joy.

By the end of the day, Lily had sold all her cookies. The money she raised was donated to a local charity. She felt a sense of accomplishment and learned the joy of sharing and giving.

From that day, Lily baked more often and shared her cookies with friends, neighbors, and anyone who needed a bit of sweetness in their lives. And even though her cookies were just a small thing, they brought a lot of happiness to people around her.

Highlighted Words:

- Mixing: Combining ingredients together.

- Decorating: Making something look attractive.

- Bake sale: An event where baked goods are sold to raise money for a cause.

- Measured: Determined the size, amount, or degree of something.

- Baking tray: A flat metal or glass pan used for baking.

- Oven: A heated compartment for baking or roasting food.

- Cookie stand: A table or booth where cookies are displayed for sale.

17. "The Neighborhood Cleanup"

In a small, **quiet** town lived a group of **spirited** children who were the best of friends. They loved to play in the park, ride their bicycles, and have fun. The leader of the group was a smart boy named Max.

One day, while playing in the park, Max noticed that there were many pieces of trash on the ground. There were empty bottles, plastic bags, and wrappers. Max felt sad. "Our beautiful park is turning into a **dump**," he thought.

Max had an idea. He gathered all his friends and said, "We must **clean up** our park. Let's organize a neighborhood cleanup!" Everyone **agreed**. They were all eager to make their park clean and beautiful again.

The next day, the children came to the park with gloves, trash bags, and big smiles. They split into small groups and started picking up the trash. The work was hard, but the children did not **complain**. They knew they were doing something important.

After many hours of work, the park was finally clean. All the trash was gone, and the park looked beautiful again. The children felt very proud of their work. They had made a difference!

That day, the children learned a valuable lesson. They learned about the importance of taking care of the environment. They understood that keeping their surroundings clean was everyone's responsibility. They promised each other that they would never throw trash on the ground again.

From then on, the children organized a neighborhood cleanup every month. Not only did they keep their park clean, but they also cleaned the streets and other public places in their town. The townspeople admired their effort and joined them in their mission.

The story of the neighborhood cleanup spread to other towns. People were inspired by the children's initiative and started organizing cleanups in their own neighborhoods. The small act of a group of children had a big impact, reminding everyone about the importance of taking care of our planet.

Highlighted Words:

- Quiet: Making very little or no noise

- Spirited: Full of energy and courage

- Dump: A place where unwanted waste is taken

- Cleanup: The act of making a place clean and tidy

- Agreed: Had the same opinion about something

- Complain - To say that something is wrong or not satisfactory

18. The Unexpected Guest

One sunny day in a small town, a **kind-hearted** family lived in a pretty blue house. The family consisted of a dad named Tom, a mom named Lisa, and two children, Mike and Sarah. They were always known for helping others in their neighborhood.

One morning, as Lisa was making breakfast, she heard a soft whimpering sound outside the front door. Opening it, she found a little, brown dog sitting on their doorstep. It was a cute dog with bright eyes and a fluffy tail, but it looked scared and **lost**.

"Kids, come here!" Lisa called. Mike and Sarah rushed to the front door. When they saw the little dog, they were **surprised**. "Where did he come from?" asked Mike. "He seems lost," Sarah added.

The family decided to take care of the little dog until they could find his owner. They gave him food and water, a warm bath, and a soft blanket to sleep on. The kids named him "Buddy" and spent time playing with him.

Days passed, and the family started growing **fond** of Buddy. He was friendly and **playful**. He loved to chase balls in the garden and curl up on their laps during movie nights. But they knew they had to find his real owner.

Tom made posters with Buddy's picture and their contact information, which they put up around town. After a week, they received a phone call. It was an old lady named Mrs. Green. She had been looking for her lost dog, who looked just like Buddy.

Mrs. Green came to their house and was overjoyed to see Buddy. Buddy wagged his tail excitedly upon seeing her. It was clear that Buddy was her dog. The family was a little sad but happy to see Buddy reunited with his real owner.

Mrs. Green was very grateful to the family for taking such good care of Buddy. She thanked them and promised that they could visit Buddy anytime they wanted.

In the end, the family learned about the importance of kindness and empathy towards animals. They realized that every animal deserves a loving home. They felt good knowing they had helped Buddy and made a new friend in Mrs. Green.

Highlighted Words:

- Kind-hearted: Caring, nice, and generous.

- Lost: Not knowing where you are.

- Surprised: Unexpectedly shocked or amazed.

- Fond: To like someone or something very much.

- Playful: Fun-loving, enjoys playing.

19. The Best Christmas Ever

It was a **frigid** winter in the small town of Northbridge. Everywhere you looked, homes were **festooned** with Christmas lights, and snowflakes were gently falling from the sky. In one of the houses, the Taylor family was getting ready for Christmas.

The Taylor family had four members: Mom, Dad, Emily, who was 10, and her younger brother, Billy, who was 7. This year, money was **tight**, and they could not afford to buy many presents. But Emily and Billy loved Christmas and were determined to make it special.

One evening, Emily had an idea. "Billy," she said, "what if we made our presents this year?" Billy thought this was an excellent idea. They decided to keep it a secret from Mom and Dad.

The following day, after school, Emily and Billy started their project. They used things they found around the house. Emily loved to draw, so she decided to make a beautiful drawing for Mom. Billy was good at making things out of paper and glue. He decided to create a model car for Dad.

Every day after school, they worked hard on their gifts. They laughed, made a mess, and had lots of fun. When Christmas Eve came, they **wrapped** their presents in old newspaper and put them under the tree.

On Christmas morning, everyone gathered around the tree. Emily and Billy could hardly contain their excitement. They handed their parents the handmade presents.

Mom opened hers first. When she saw Emily's drawing, tears welled up in her eyes. "Emily, this is beautiful," she said, hugging Emily tightly.

Dad was next. He laughed when he saw the paper car Billy made. "This is the best car I ever got," Dad said, giving Billy a big hug.

That night, as Emily and Billy went to bed, they agreed that it was the best Christmas ever. They learned that it's not about the money you spend on gifts, but the love and thoughtfulness you put into them.

And so, in their small house in Northbridge, the Taylor family had a Christmas that they would never forget. A Christmas filled with love, joy, and handmade presents.

Highlighted Words:

- Frigid: Very cold.

- Festooned: Decorated.

- Tight: Firmly or closely fixed in place.

- Wrapped: Covered by folding or winding something around.

20. The First Snowfall

In a small, **cozy** town named Fairview, there was a young boy named Timmy. Timmy was a **bright** and curious seven-year-old, always eager to explore new things. He had golden hair, bright blue eyes, and a contagious laugh that filled everyone with joy.

One day, when Timmy woke up, he noticed something strange outside his window. The entire town, usually filled with the colors of fall, had turned completely white. It was snowing! Timmy had read about snow in books and seen it in movies, but he had never seen it in person before. This was his first snowfall!

Filled with excitement, Timmy quickly put on his warmest clothes and ran outside. The cold breeze made him shiver, but he didn't mind. He was too happy to see the snow. The ground was covered with a thick blanket of snow, and more snowflakes were falling from the sky.

Timmy started to play. He made a snow angel, leaving a perfect outline of his small body in the snow. He laughed as he looked at the funny figure he had created.

Then, he decided to build a snowman. He rolled up a big snowball for the base, a smaller one for the body, and an even smaller one for the head. He found two stones for the eyes, a carrot for the nose, and **twigs** for the arms. Standing back to look at his **creation**, Timmy felt a sense of **accomplishment**.

Later, his friends from the neighborhood came over. They divided themselves into two teams and had a fun snowball fight. They laughed and played until they were all out of breath.

When the day ended, Timmy was tired but happy. He had had the best day of his life. His first snowfall had taught him that joy could be found in the simplest of things. He learned to appreciate the beauty of nature and the happiness it could bring. As he went to bed that night, he wished for more snowy days, eager to make more beautiful memories.

Highlighted Words:

- Cozy: Comfortable and warm.

- Bright: Very smart or intelligent.

- Twigs: Small thin branches of a tree or bush.

- Creation: Something that has been made or brought into existence.

- Accomplishment: Something that has been achieved successfully.

Give your honest opinion on Amazon!

Your suggestions and criticisms are invaluable.

They make every reading experience even more satisfying!

Thank you very much for reading my book.

I wish you all the success you deserve!

Printed in Great Britain
by Amazon